MW01065286

Young Heroes

Alexandra Scott

Other titles in the Young Heroes series include:

Elizabeth Bloomer, Child Labor Activist
Emmanuel Osofu Yeboah, Champion for Ghana's Disabled
James Quadrino, Wildlife Protector
Jhalak Man Tamang, Slave Labor Whistleblower
Jyotirmayee Mohapatra, Advocate for India's Young Women

Young Heroes

Alexandra Scott

Champion for Cancer Research

KIDHAVEN PRESS
An imprint of Thomson Gale, a part of The Thomson Corporation

Detroit • New York • San Diego • San Francisco
Boston • New Haven, Conn. • Waterville, Maine
London • Munich

For more information, contact
KidHaven Press
27500 Drake Rd.
Farmington Hills, MI 48331-3535
Or you can visit our Internet site at http://www.gale.com

LIBRARY OF CONGRESS CATALOGING-IN-PUBLICATION DATA

Stewart, Gail B.
Alexandra Scott / by Gail B. Stewart
p. cm. -- (Young heroes))
Includes bibliographical references and index.
Summary: Discusses the life of Alexandra Scott, her lemonade stand and how she contributed to cancer research, and how the lemonade stand for cancer research became a phenomenon.
ISBN 0-7377-3613-5 (hard cover : alk. paper) 1. Scott Alexandra, 1996-2004.
2. People with cancer—children—biography—juvenile literature. 3. People with Disabilities—children—attitudes—juvenile literature. I. Title. II. Series.

Printed in the United States of America

Contents

An Unlikely Hero

For proof that one person can make a difference in the world, one only has to look at the life of Alexandra Scott—or Alex, as she liked to be called. Very young and terminally ill with cancer, she was the unlikeliest of heroes. Yet four-year-old Alex had an idea for a way she could raise money for doctors to find a cure—not only for herself, but for all children battling cancer.

Her idea caught on in her own community, then quickly captured the attention of the nation. Over the next four years, Alex was interviewed by numerous magazines and newspapers and appeared on *Oprah*, *Today*, and several news programs. In addition, she was honored with a number of important **humanitarian** awards, such as the Philadelphia **Philanthropist** of the Year and the Philadelphia 76ers Hometown Hero Award.

No one, it seemed, could believe that such a young girl, sick with cancer from the time she was an infant, could have accomplished so much in her short life. They wondered how she could have thought up a fund-raising idea so utterly simple yet so amazingly successful. By the time Alex died, at age eight, she had raised hundreds of thousands of dollars for fighting children's cancers, and the foundation in her

Alex Scott takes part in an Alex's Lemonade Stand fund-raiser at her school in June 2004, just two months before her death from cancer.

name has continued to fund cancer research. A little more than two years after her death, the foundation had raised more than $6 million.

A Fussy Baby

Alexandra Flynn Scott was born on January 18, 1996, in Hartford, Connecticut. Her parents, Liz and Jay Scott, were delighted that they had a new daughter—a sister for their little boy, Patrick. However, Liz Scott recalls, she

The Philadelphia 76ers present Alex (center) with their Hometown Hero Award in 2002.

and her husband became concerned about Alex's health when she was still a baby:

> She was losing weight, and that's very unusual for a baby. Babies are supposed to do a lot of growing during their first year, but Alex wasn't. She was also very, very irritable. She'd cry and want to be held. For most babies, this time of their life is when they are crawling around, exploring their world, wanting to play. But Alex just wanted to be held. It just didn't seem right.[1]

Sleeping was very difficult for Alex, too. She would go to sleep but wake up every half hour or so and scream and cry, again wanting to be held. Of course, her parents knew that all babies cry, but Alex's crying seemed a symptom of something more serious.

Alex's doctor examined her several times, but found no cause for alarm. "He said she was just a miserable child," recalls Liz Scott. "He called it 'failure to thrive,' and said that she would eventually grow out of it. It was very frustrating, though, because Jay and I felt that there was more to it than that. It just didn't make any sense to us. There had to be a reason that she was eating so much, yet not gaining any weight."[2]

Devastating News

Finally, two days before Alex's first birthday, doctors did an **MRI scan**—a special test that allowed them to see inside Alex's body without performing surgery. The scan showed a large **tumor** in her abdomen, pressing against her spine.

The doctors suspected that the tumor was a form of cancer called **neuroblastoma** However, it was not possible to be completely sure until they could do a **biopsy**—a procedure in which a small cutting of the tumor is studied under the microscope. On Alex's first birthday, doctors performed surgery, removing as much of the tumor as they could, and sent a cutting of it to the laboratory for analysis.

The biopsy showed that the tumor was cancerous. This was devastating news for the Scotts. Liz Scott says that she had had a feeling that whatever was wrong with Alex was serious. The diagnosis of cancer was a shock, however. "It was her first birthday," recalls Scott. "I thought, what does she have ahead of her? What kind of life is she going to have?"[3]

But while the news made Alex's parents sad, Liz Scott says, at least they finally knew what had been causing their daughter so much discomfort. Now they could focus on helping her get better.

Waiting and Watching

The Scotts learned that neuroblastoma, the type of cancer Alex had, is a disease that affects infants and small children. It is an aggressive cancer that starts in the developing nerve cells and spreads to the bones and other parts of the body. No one knows the cause of neuroblastoma.

The doctors told the Scotts that they were able to remove about 99 percent of the tumor. It could grow back, they said, but there was also a possibility that any cancer cells left in her body would stop growing. This

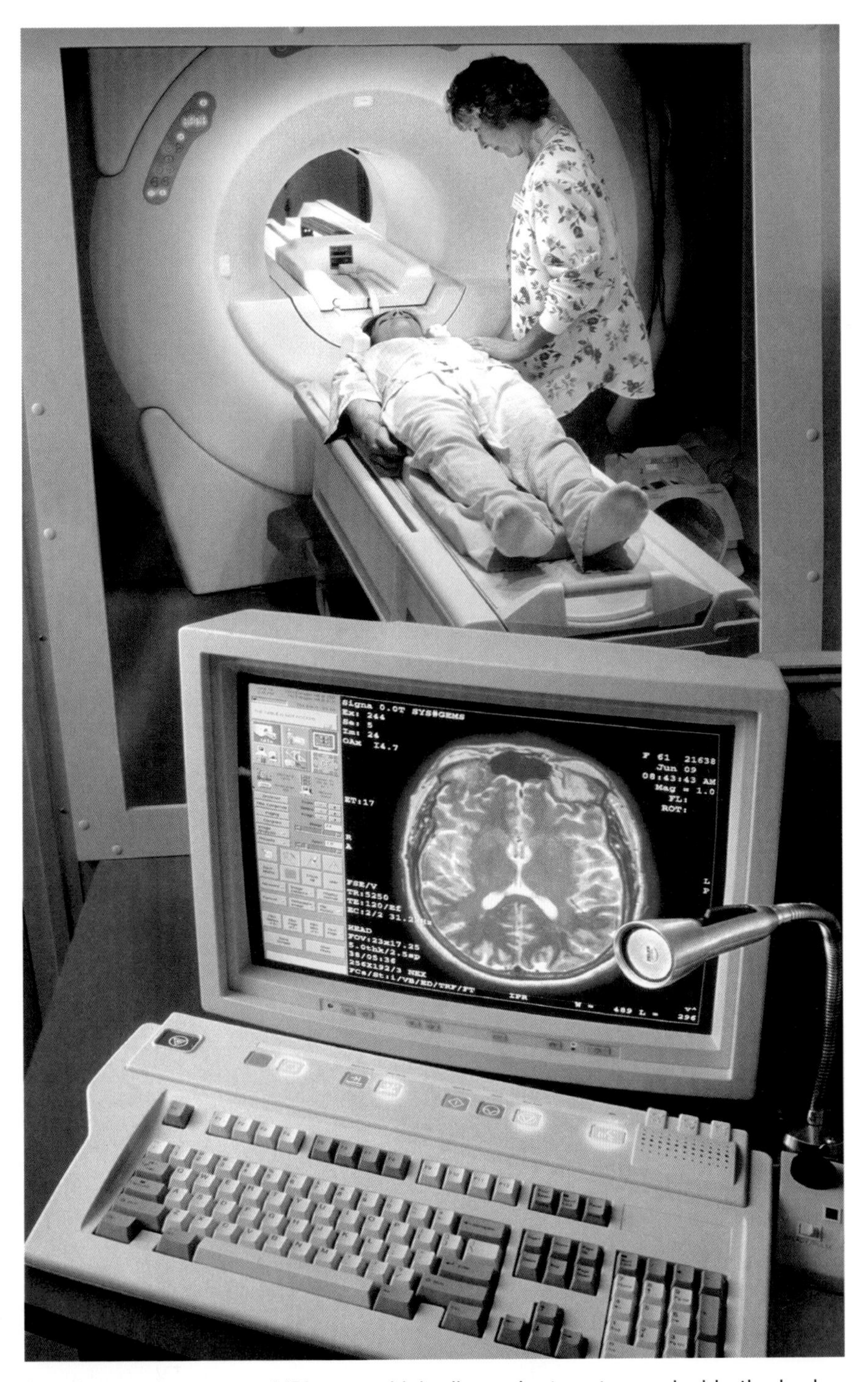

A patient undergoes an MRI scan which allows doctors to see inside the body.

occasionally happens with cancers in very young children. "What we did was wait," says her mother. "We took her in for scans every couple of months, and hoped for the best—that as the doctors monitored the situation, they would see no sign that the tumor was growing back."[4]

Life on Chemotherapy

However, by the time Alex was two, doctors could see that the tumor was growing, so it was necessary to begin treating the cancer. Alex began the traditional therapies doctors use to fight the disease. One was **radia-**

A boy with leukemia bears the most common mark of chemotherapy, a bald head.

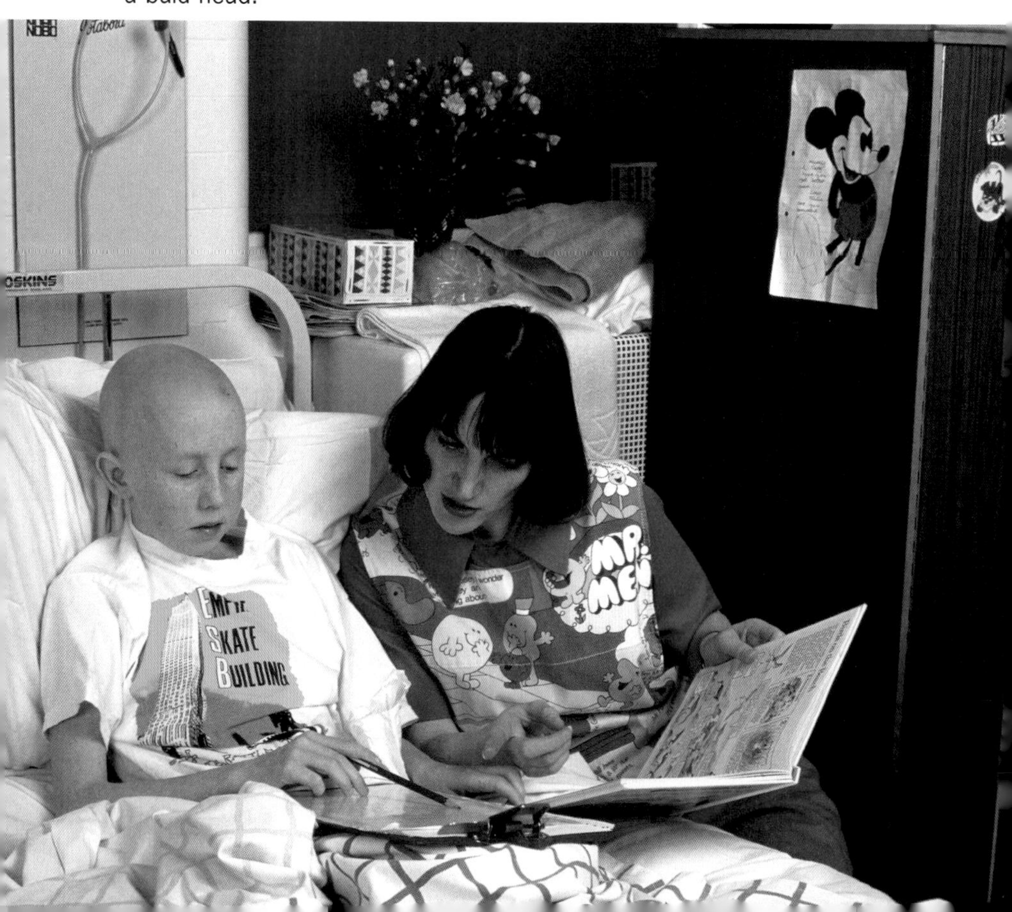

tion therapy, in which doctors used high-energy X-rays to try to shrink her tumor. She also underwent **chemotherapy** in which she took special medicines that would kill cancer cells in her body.

Chemotherapy is usually difficult, for the strong drugs can cause a number of unpleasant side effects. They can make the patient sick to the stomach and very tired. In addition, chemotherapy drugs kill some of a patient's healthy cells along with cancerous ones. Cancer patients often temporarily lose their hair while they are on chemotherapy.

Alex's mother recalls that Alex coped well with chemotherapy when she was little. Says Liz Scott:

> And as far as her hair falling out—she was so young, she didn't worry about losing her hair, like an older kid would. It fell out, and when she'd finish a round of chemo, it would grow back. It didn't matter. And when Alex was feeling sick, she didn't dwell on it. She would feel bad for a while, and then she'd feel better and things would get back to normal.[5]

A Victory

As she went through the radiation therapy and chemotherapy meant to fight her cancer, Alex accomplished something her doctors had predicted would never happen: She learned to walk. When the doctors had removed the tumor when she was a year old, they had been forced to remove a small part of her spine as well. At the time, the surgeons told the Scotts that it

Alex enjoys a quiet moment on a beautiful fall day, relaxing with a sketchpad and colored pencils.

would be unlikely that their daughter would ever walk, because she had no feeling in her legs.

But Alex was determined. She struggled to pull herself to a standing position and began to take steps. She often fell, but she got up again and kept trying. She was fitted for leg braces, and she continued her struggle to walk by herself. Her mother says that Alex's accomplishment astonished everyone.

"I still can't imagine how she did it," she says. "The **physical therapist** was always amazed, too. How could anyone, without any sensation in their legs, balance and walk? It seems impossible—how do you feel the ground? But she did it."[6] The Scotts wondered if neuroblastoma could be conquered with that same determination.

"Maybe They'll Find a Cure"

Even with a child fighting a life-threatening disease, the Scott family settled into a routine. Alex went to her various doctor visits and chemotherapy sessions. When the chemo damaged her blood cells, she went into the hospital for transfusions.

When she was not doing any of those things, she was being a normal little girl in a loving, busy family. She enjoyed puzzles and stuffed animals. She liked to play with dolls and design clothes for them. She also liked books, television, movies, and—cancer or no cancer—she enjoyed physical activities.

Her father says that it was not Alex's personality to sit on the sidelines and watch. She would much rather participate. "She certainly didn't let [her cancer] slow her down when she was young," says her father. "If we were playing a game of catch, she tried to get in there and take the ball away from her older brother and me."[7]

Difficult Times

But there was a lot of time spent at the hospital getting treatments. "It was heartbreaking," remembers her mother. "For us, it was a lot of holding her, a lot of sleeping with her—especially when she had to spend

Alex (left) and her brothers practice their karate punches.

nights in the hospital for an infection or some other problem. She'd rather have been home. Those were long nights."[8]

By the time she was four years old, Alex had spent a lot of time at the hospital in West Hartford. She saw how many other children with cancer were in the same hospital. Some were in far more serious shape than she was. She wondered what would happen to all of them.

She knew that neuroblastoma was not the only kind of cancer that affected children. She also understood that while many children did survive cancer, many did not. Too many things about cancer were unknown to doctors. Hospitals could only do so much to cure patients. Without the right medicine and the right therapies, many children were bound to die, and that troubled her.

An Idea

After one of her treatments in the hospital, four-year-old Alex announced to her mother that she had an idea. She wanted to have a lemonade stand to raise money. When her mother asked what she wanted to buy with the money she would make, Alex said that the money was not for herself. She explained that she wanted it to go to her hospital and her doctors. Says Scott, "Alex's thought was, 'If I make extra money through a lemonade stand to donate to the hospital, maybe they'll find a cure for me and all the sick kids with cancer.'"[9]

Scott admits that she was not **optimistic** about raising much money with a lemonade stand. "I thought the idea was cute," she says. "But I didn't think it would be

Four-year-old Alex Scott launches her first lemonade stand to raise money for cancer research.

a major fund-raising effort. I thought she would give her doctor five or ten dollars."[10] When she told her daughter that it would be hard to raise much money selling lemonade for 50 cents a cup, Alex replied, "I don't care. I'll do it anyway."[11]

Getting Dressed Before Going to Bed

Alex decided that she would also sell some of her toys at her lemonade stand. She and Patrick chose some puzzles, old stuffed animals, and a few dolls that were in good shape. She then gathered the supplies she would need to sell lemonade—cups, ice, sugar, and lots of fresh lemons.

As her daughter was organizing her fund-raising efforts, Scott got on the phone with relatives who lived nearby. She told them about Alex's plan and urged them to drop over the next morning so her daughter would have at least a few customers.

The night before, Alex got dressed in her favorite tank top and shorts to save time the following morning. Although the stand was not due to open until 8:00 A.M., she was too excited to sleep. She got up and had her leg braces on before 6:00 A.M., happy because the big day had come.

A Beautiful Stand

The stand, complete with large, colorfully painted signs proclaiming "Alex's Lemonade Stand—To Benefit **Pediatric** Cancer Research," looked beautiful. Alex's father had set up a picnic table with Alex's little toy cash register on the front lawn. There were stacks of paper cups

A five-year-old boy whose brother suffered from cancer helps out at an Alex's Lemonade Stand in Minneapolis in 2004.

and a large cooler of lemonade Alex had taste-tested herself. In a comfortable chair behind the table, she waited for her first customers.

If Liz Scott worried that her daughter would not have many customers that day, those worries soon evaporated. Relatives came, and so did neighbors. Someone had called the local newspaper, which sent a reporter to cover the event. Over the next hours, news of Alex's stand spread by word of mouth, and the front yard was crowded with people.

Though the sign said that the lemonade was 50 cents a cup, many people gave far more. They were impressed by the little girl who was raising money—not for herself, but for the good of all children with cancer. Some customers gave ten- or twenty-dollar bills and waved away their change. One man gave $100 and wrote a note saying, "I want you to know that I think your homemade lemonade stand is the BEST! Your mom and dad must be very proud of you. I am, too."[12]

Inspired by Alex Scott, young volunteers in Puerto Rico join the Alex's Lemonade Stand campaign in 2005.

Maybe Next Year

Alex enjoyed working at the stand, chatting with customers and helping cut lemon slices to put on the rim of each cup. However, after two hours, **fatigue**—a side effect of chemotherapy—overwhelmed her, and she went inside to rest. Alex was amazed at how many customers had come. She told her mother, "I haven't had five minutes to myself."[13] Her family took over for her.

When it was time to close the stand, Alex helped count the money she had raised. During its three hours of business, Alex's stand had raised an unbelievable $2,000 for cancer research and her hospital. Someone asked Liz Scott if she thought Alex would have another stand sometime in the future. "We may do it again next year if she wants one," she replied. "I am just hoping that we won't be using their services quite as much."[14]

Sad Advice

But while Alex and her family tried to be hopeful about beating her cancer, they knew that the tumor was not going away. Despite the rounds of chemotherapy, radiation, and other traditional methods of fighting her neuroblastoma, doctors at her West Hartford hospital were not seeing the results they had hoped for. Many children do respond to such treatments, and their cancers go into remission—a state in which the cancer may not disappear but stops growing and causing symptoms. But in Alex's case, there was no remission.

"Alex's doctors told us that there was more they could do, but it wouldn't cure her," recalls Liz Scott. "So after treating her for so many years, they advised that we should stop treating her. They thought it would be better to give her some time away from the hospital."[15]

But the Scotts did not agree. "Alex was still doing well—she was very active, doing lots of fun things," says Liz Scott. "We didn't feel that she was at the point where she was ready to give up."[16]

Instead, they consulted doctors from Children's Hospital of Philadelphia, where a number of experimental cancer treatments were being tried. Those doctors felt that they could certainly do experimental therapies that would extend Alex's life, even though a cure

The Scott family turned to doctors at Children's Hospital of Philadelphia (pictured) for the latest treatments.

was doubtful. Most important, they indicated that Alex would have a good quality of life while she was participating in these studies.

The family decided to move to Wynnewood, Pennsylvania, a suburb of Philadelphia, to be close to the hospital there. It was hard for the family to leave Connecticut. They had relatives and many dear friends there. But Philadelphia was where Alex's new hospital was, and that was where they all needed to be.

Chapter Three

The Idea Grows

Alex began her new treatments in Philadelphia, and for a time she did very well. She liked her doctors and got into the routine of chemotherapy, tests, scans, and other appointments. Though some of the procedures were experimental, they caused many of the same side effects she had experienced before—including fatigue and upset stomach.

"More Fun than Anybody"

But typically, Alex endured the side effects without much complaint. Most of the time she could receive her treatments during the day and go home afterward. Her father says that just as when she was very young, Alex was able to bounce back from the discomfort quickly. "When she was having fun, she had more fun than anybody you could imagine," he says. "She was the type of kid who would go to the hospital, get a treatment, get sick and throw up, and come home and eat nachos."[17]

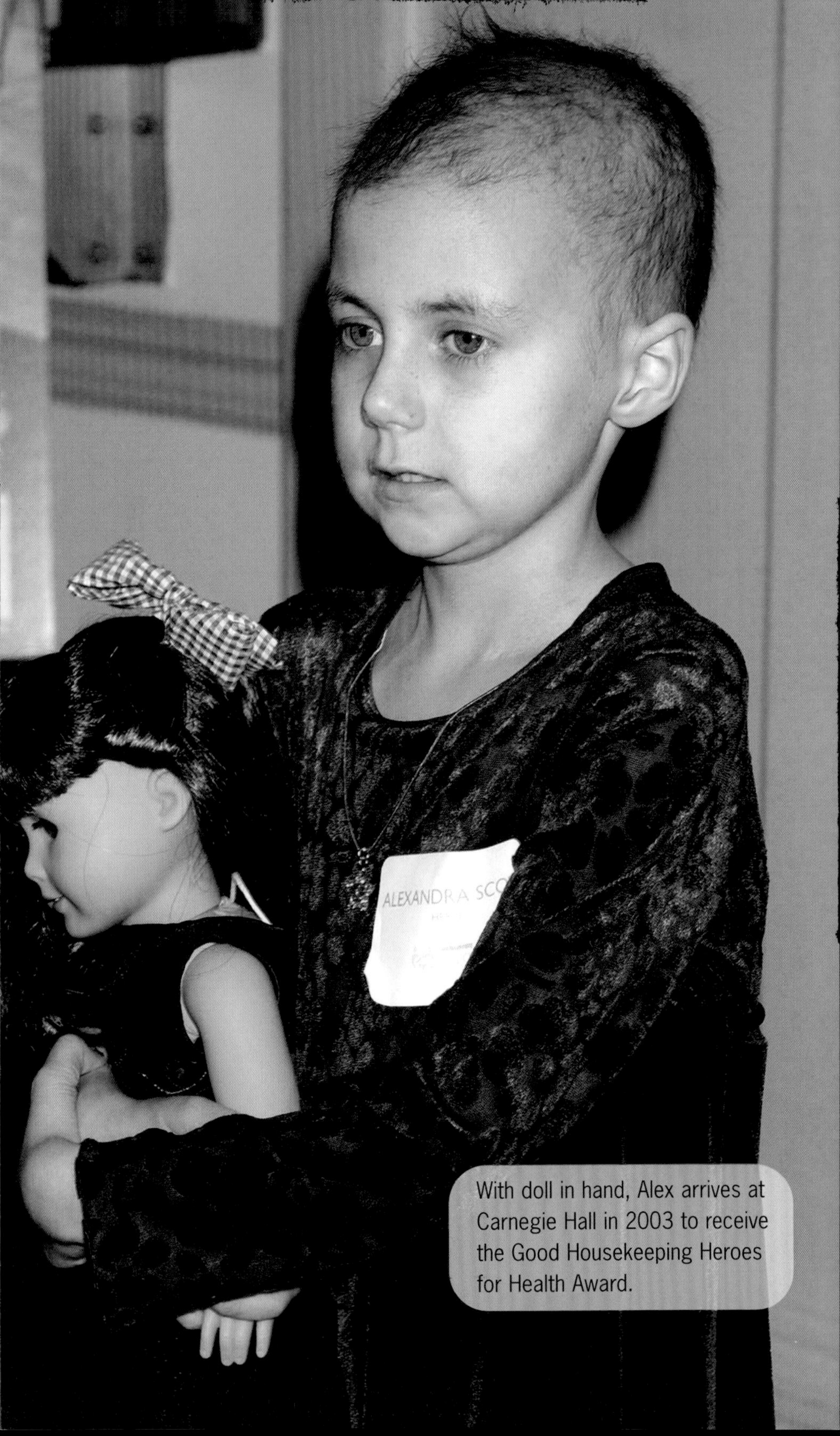

With doll in hand, Alex arrives at Carnegie Hall in 2003 to receive the Good Housekeeping Heroes for Health Award.

Liz Scott agrees. "She loved to laugh, to have fun. She did all the things other little girls her age would do—play with American Girl dolls, eat french fries, watch *Shrek* movies, watch *American Idol* on TV. She didn't dwell on the cancer when she wasn't having treatments, and that was good."[18]

Alex's lack of anxiety might have been because her family treated her treatment schedules—even the unexpected problems that sometimes resulted in a visit to the emergency room—as a normal way of life. Her little brothers—Eddie, born in 1999, and Joey, born in 2003—often accompanied their mother to the hospital's dayroom. There, they felt very much at home while

Like other kids her age, Alex liked to ride her bike.

their sister was having treatments or a blood transfusion. "This may sound weird," her father once told reporters, "but we're all used to her treatments. It's what she knows, it's what we know."[19]

Alex especially enjoyed another aspect of life in her new home—going to school. She was a quick learner, and she loved to make new friends. When she was in the early grades, her condition was fairly good, and she was able to attend school about half the time. She missed school when she had chemotherapy each month and when she needed to go in for blood work. When she had to miss class for an extended time, she was taught by a teacher who came to her home.

The Idea Grows

One thing Alex brought with her from Connecticut was her lemonade stand fund-raising plan. She hoped to make even more money and to donate some of it to her new hospital. While she operated her stand in Wynnewood, her relatives and friends back in West Hartford kept her stand going there, too. By the age of six, Alex had collected more than $18,000 for children's cancer research.

She also received a great deal of media attention for her accomplishments. She was interviewed by a number of newspapers and magazines. In November 2002, she was given the Philadelphia 76ers Hometown Hero Award for her fund-raising efforts. This publicity called attention to the cause of children's cancer. Many people wanted to help raise more money for Alex's fund by operating lemonade stands of their own.

Her mother and father got involved, too. They made formal arrangements for Alex's charity so that people could send in donations without having to visit the lemonade stand. The name of the charity was Alex's Lemonade Stand Foundation, and its motto was "Fighting Childhood Cancer One Cup at a Time." There was a Web site, too, so children and adults could learn about childhood cancer or even get information about organizing their own lemonade stand. Alex's idea was growing quickly, and that meant more and more money was coming in to fight children's cancer.

Failing Health

But as her charity was blooming, Alex's health was failing. By the time she was seven years old, the cancer had spread close to one kidney, to her liver, and to one of her lungs. She often suffered painful headaches and missed more and more school because she needed more treatments and blood transfusions at the hospital.

Even so, Alex continued to be as active as she could. She enjoyed doing things with her brothers—including her new baby brother, Joey. She played with her new puppy, which she named Shammy (short for Shamrock). She learned to knit, and when she felt well enough, she even took karate lessons with Patrick and Eddie.

She took pleasure in planning her lemonade stands, too. In 2003, when she held her stand in Philadelphia, children in a number at other cities were doing the same thing. Businesses got involved, too. The Volvo Car company offered to allow Alex's Lemonade Stands

Young people (and adults) have honored Alex's efforts by setting up Alex's lemonade stands.

at their dealerships. By the end of that summer, Alex's Lemonade Stand Foundation had raised over $80,000, and more and more people wanted to get involved. It seemed that Alex's idea was growing faster than she had ever imagined.

A Million Dollars?

Alex told her parents that her goal for 2004 was for her fund to reach $1 million. The foundation was receiving contributions from businesses as well as individuals, and she believed it could happen. Before June 12—lemonade stand day—eight-year-old Alex appeared on both *Oprah*

Carl's Commandos, named for Carl Robinson, raised money in Minneapolis. Carl had the same form of cancer as Alex.

and the *Today* show. It was hard for her, for she did not feel well, and recent radiation and chemotherapy treatments had made her weak. Even so, she did it, because she knew it would help get word of the fund to more people. And when June 12 came, the Scotts learned that there were more than 500 other lemonade stands, at least one in every state, as well as France and Ontario, Canada.

Alex's own stand that year was to be held at her grade school, Penn Wynne Elementary. Her classmates had organized booths with food, games, and music for the day. Alex could only put in an appearance at her stand, however, because she was not feeling well.

Even so, she was very excited about the day. She sat in a wheelchair, looking very small and pale. Her mother pushed her around the school yard. "I'm just proud of her for being here," said Scott. "It's overwhelming for her—people love her and want to be near her. She's not saying much, but she's very excited."[20]

The results that day were amazing. The stand in Wynnewood raised $36,000—not including $22,000 in donations that came in before the stand even opened. Alex's idea, which had begun when she was four years old, had raised a total of more than $200,000 for children's cancer research. And that total grew as people who had lemonade stands in other places sent in their money, too.

"She Did Well for a Very Long Time"

But while the Scotts were proud of their daughter's accomplishments, they knew that Alex was dying. She had been through a great deal—6 surgeries to try to remove

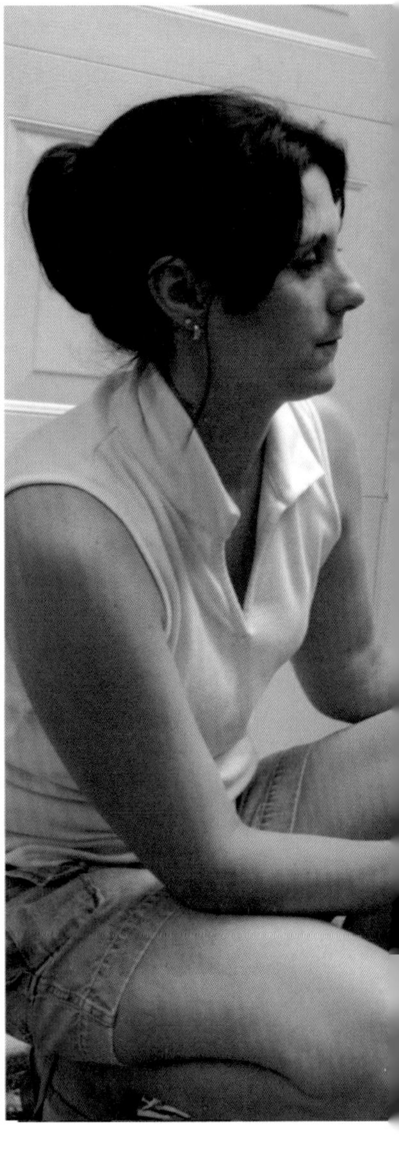

tumors, more than 600 **out-patient** visits to hospitals, 40 rounds of chemotherapy, and 7 radiation treatments. But the cancer was winning, and even the experimental therapies were no longer helping.

"We had known for several weeks that the end was near," says her mother. "It was as though Alex had been determined to go to that last lemonade stand day at the school, and after that, she was satisfied."[21]

On August 1, 2004, less than two months after that day, Alex died at home with her mother and father. "She went as peacefully as we could have hoped," says Liz Scott. "She just slipped away. . . . You could see when she was ready. . . . I feel very fortunate that we had her at home and she wasn't in the hospital, hooked up to **intravenous** drips."[22]

At her funeral, Alex's parents disputed the idea that cancer had beaten their daughter. They said:

> So many times this week, we have heard people say that Alex lost her battle with cancer. We be-

Liz Scott helps Alex and her brother Eddie build one of Alex's famous lemonade stands.

lieve that this could not be farther from the truth. Alex won her battle in so many ways . . . by facing her cancer everyday but still managing to smile; by making the most of every moment; by never giving up hope; by living life to the fullest; and by leaving an incredible legacy of hope and inspiration for all of us.

We are proud of her; We love her; We are grateful for her life; We will miss her.[23]

Alex's Legacy

Alex's death did not mean the end of her work. The Alex's Lemonade Stand Foundation was still in place, and people were still donating money to fight children's cancer. In fact, soon after Alex died, the Volvo corporation announced a plan to make her goal of raising $1 million a reality. Within three months of Alex's death, her foundation's fundraising had topped the million dollar mark, and it has grown steadily since then. Her parents have worked hard to continue the foundation's work.

A Four-Legged Supporter

Some large donations have come from businesses and corporations. Some have come from civic organizations, such as the Kiwanis Club and various scouting groups. But one of the most unusual donors was a racehorse!

His name was Afleet Alex, and he was owned by a group of men who lived in the Philadelphia area. (Some people mistakenly thought that the horse was named after Alex Scott, but he was really named after one of the owner's sons.) The owners heard about Alex's fund-raising, and they were saddened to hear of her death in 2004.

They decided to help her cause both by donating thousands of dollars to the fund and by giving a percentage of the horse's prize money for each race he won. To show their support of the Alex's Lemonade Stand Foundation, the owners decided to have lemon-shaped patches sewn on Afleet Alex's saddle blanket and the jockey's clothes for each race. They hoped that would call attention to Alex's fund to fight children's cancer. In addition, they urged racetracks all around the country to hold lemonade stands for Alex's fund.

A Stumble, but No Fall

Afleet Alex was incredibly fast and won important races in the spring of 2005. In the Preakness—one of the three most famous races in the United States—he almost fell when he and another horse collided. He regained his balance, however, and somehow managed to win the race as the crowd cheered.

Liz and Jay Scott were watching the race and were struck then by the similarity between the two Alexes. Liz Scott remembered that from the time she was very young, Alex wore leg braces as she tried to walk. Her right leg would sometimes give out, and she would stumble.

"But she'd pop right back up," she recalled. "Amazing. And when Afleet Alex stumbled and almost fell . . . and then got himself together—and not only finished the race unharmed, but won it, we were reminded of

Afleet Alex and his jockey wore lemon-shaped patches in support of Alex Scott's efforts.

Afleet Alex wins the Preakness in 2005 despite stumbling during the race.

Alex. How she battled back. There were tears in our eyes."[24] It somehow seemed right that Afleet Alex was helping Alex Scott's cause.

So Many Kinds of Lemonade Stands

The media attention Afleet Alex brought to Alex's foundation made more people aware that the work Alex had begun would continue. In the summer of 2005, there were more lemonade stands than ever before—more than 1,000 across North America. And there was great variety in the people who set up stands and in their reasons for doing so.

Some were children who were interested in the story of Alex's life. One Virginia fourth grader named Hailey read a newspaper story about Alex, who was exactly her age—eight years old—when she died. Hailey was inspired by the story and decided to make her own stand. In the process, she raised more than $200. Hailey plans to open her stand again soon and hopes to sell some of her toys, as Alex did at her first stand. Though Hailey says she does not know anyone with cancer, Alex's story made her sad. "She should not have died," says Hailey, "because she was only eight years old."[25]

Many others who have had stands know firsthand what cancer can do. One Connecticut woman raised more than $1,000 for Alex's fund at her lemonade stand. She explained that she was doing it as a way of helping her grandson, who had been diagnosed recently with neuroblastoma.

In California, opening a lemonade stand was a way for two parents to grieve for their sixteen-month-old son, who had also suffered from neuroblastoma. They admitted that the only thing that would give them joy, since their son had died, was to witness a cure for other children with cancer. "One year will have passed since the death of our beautiful son, Lorenzo Bla Rissolo," they wrote in a letter to friends announcing their lemonade stand. "It will be a day to share with our family, our friends, and with Alexandra 'Alex' Scott and her lemonade stand. . . . Though we have only the memory of our little Enzo beside us, we are inspired to do our small part."[26]

What Money Will Buy

The Scotts are proud of the thousands of people who have set up lemonade stands. They are especially glad that the Alex's Lemonade Stand Foundation has already made a difference by asking researchers and hospitals what they need to fight cancer. Liz and Jay Scott, as well as the others working for the foundation, want the money to be used on new treatments that will help sick children now, not just years down the line.

One of the problems hospitals noticed was how long it can take for doctors and families to enroll a child in an experimental therapy. There is so much paperwork involved that it slows down the process. That means that the child loses valuable time waiting for new treatments. Money from Alex's foundation has been used to hire hospital workers whose job is to help speed the process along.

Some of the foundation money goes to men and women who are working on cures and new therapies.

A researcher continues work toward understanding neuroblastoma and finding a cure.

In 2005, eight full-time research positions for people working on cures for children's cancer were funded by Alex's Lemonade Stand money. And more ideas are being proposed every day.

Getting Involved

Though a great deal is being accomplished in fighting the different types of children's cancer, experts are still far from being able to cure them. In fact, more and more children are being diagnosed in the United States each year. In 2006, it was likely that one in every four schools in the country had at least one student who had cancer. Cancer is the leading cause of death of children aged fifteen and younger.

Many people who hear about Alex's life decide they want to help by having their own lemonade stand. But there are many other valuable ways that young people can get involved in the fight against children's cancer, too.

Giving the World a Great Present

Alex saw that many children were sick, and she wanted to help by giving money to researchers and hospitals. A new therapy or even a cure would benefit all children with cancer. Raising money for such research is an important job.

An Alex's Lemonade Stand fund-raiser at Penn Wynne Elementary School, where Alex was a student, attracts many visitors and volunteers.

Some young people have become involved in another way. Fourteen-year-old Tracy, whose younger brother Ryan died of neuroblastoma when he was three, says she wants to be a researcher herself when she grows up. She and her family learned a lot about the disease when Ryan was sick, and she wants to learn even more. Tracy explains:

> When I was younger, the idea of cancer didn't really scare me, but it made me angry. I thought about Ryan, and how bad he felt, and how no one could make him better. When I got to eighth grade, I did a project on neuroblastoma for my science class. Then my teacher talked to me about being a doctor or a researcher.
>
> She said that since I'm good in science, that it might be a good way to honor Ryan's memory. I'd go to a medical school, and then do lots of research in a laboratory. I'd try to come up with a way to cure all of those kids. It wouldn't be easy, I know. I'd work on it for a long time—maybe until I'm old. But if I could do it, I'd feel like I gave the world a great present.[27]

"Nurses Are the Greatest"

Some young cancer survivors, such as sixteen-year-old Jordan, say that their own fight with cancer has given them ideas about how to get involved. She had leukemia, a cancer of the blood, when she was nine. She was very sick, and, like Alex Scott, had a lot of chemotherapy. Jordan says:

I don't have cancer anymore. I am in high school, but I remember those days in the hospital. I got so sick from chemo, and I got scared. I remember the nurses on the third floor, where the kids with cancer were, and how great they were. They'd sit with me and make me feel like I should have hope. They didn't mind when I was bratty and crabby. They knew it was because I was sick, and they didn't get mad.

A doctor comforts a young cancer patient.

> From the time I was ten or eleven, I knew that's what I wanted to be when I grow up, and I haven't changed my mind. Curing cancer is the best idea, but until then, nurses are the greatest.[28]

But What About Right Now?

While such future goals are important, there are ways to help now. One is to maintain contact with a classmate who is going through cancer treatment. Many children with cancer say that they often feel cut off from their friends and schoolmates.

"You spend so much time in the hospital," says one boy. "At first guys on [my basketball team] would call and talk to my mom, and ask her how I was. I didn't call back sometimes, because I was sick from chemo, or whatever. And, I don't know, I just didn't feel like I was part of the team anymore."[29]

Some students have made a difference by staying connected with classmates that are ill. They send e-mails, cards, and even videos of activities they are doing and let their friend know they are thinking about him or her. Says Lila, a mother of a boy with cancer:

> It's a little thing, but it really makes a difference. The kids use the computer in the library

at school and send him messages. Josh checks his e-mail six or seven times a day and instant messages back and forth with these kids. IM stuff used to drive me crazy before he got sick—I thought, what a waste of time. Now, I think, it's an amazing tool—letting kids who spend so much time alone feel included.[30]

Making a Day Spa

One challenge faced by many cancer patients is dealing with the temporary change in appearance that can make them feel embarrassed around other people.

Young people being treated for cancer try to have normal lives even when daily life seems far from normal.

Chemotherapy causes them to lose their hair, and certain drugs may also give them a rash or make them gain weight, especially in their faces. Even though such side effects eventually go away, they can make patients uncomfortable.

To help young cancer patients with this aspect of their illness, one group of high school girls got permission to have a day spa for children going through chemotherapy. One of the girls, Sara, explains:

A teenager who has cancer finds simple things like brushing her hair improves her outlook and how she feels about herself.

> Mostly we did manicures and pedicures. We had like fifty different colors of nail polish, and lots of emery boards and hand lotion. We brought a bunch of bandanas for kids who had lost their hair, too.
>
> We visited about nine girls—from about age eight or nine up to thirteen, I guess. We joked around and gave hand massages and did their nails. They really liked it. I don't know that we were very good, but they had fun. And I know it wasn't about us—but really, it was a good feeling, knowing that just for a half hour or so, I made someone feel good, even though they're going through some bad days.[31]

Asked if she would do it again, Sara did not hesitate. "Oh, yeah—I'd do it again in a second,"[32] she says.

Not Only the Sick Kids

While volunteers like Sara focus an helping young cancer patients, others try to aid the patients' families. When a child has cancer, his or her whole family is affected. Some of the most thoughtful ways to help out involve not just the person who is ill, but his or her brothers or sisters. They often need attention, too, especially when parents spend lots of time at the hospital.

Thirteen-year-old Marissa found a way to help a family from her church whose three-year-old daughter had cancer. The little girl had two older sisters, aged six and nine. The mother of the girls spent a great deal of time at the hospital, but taking the two girls with her was difficult.

"I offered to babysit for them for free," says Marissa. "I did it for about four weeks, three times a week. It was fun—we read stories, baked brownies, played video games. I think they had fun coming over to my house instead of going to the hospital with their mom."[33]

The Most Important Legacy of All

However they choose to help those affected by childhood cancer, many people have been inspired by Alex Scott. After all, she accomplished a great deal in her eight years of life. She dealt with a painful disease bravely. In addition, she found an amazing way to raise money for a cause that would fight pediatric cancer.

But the most important thing her life shows is that one person can make a great difference in the world. A

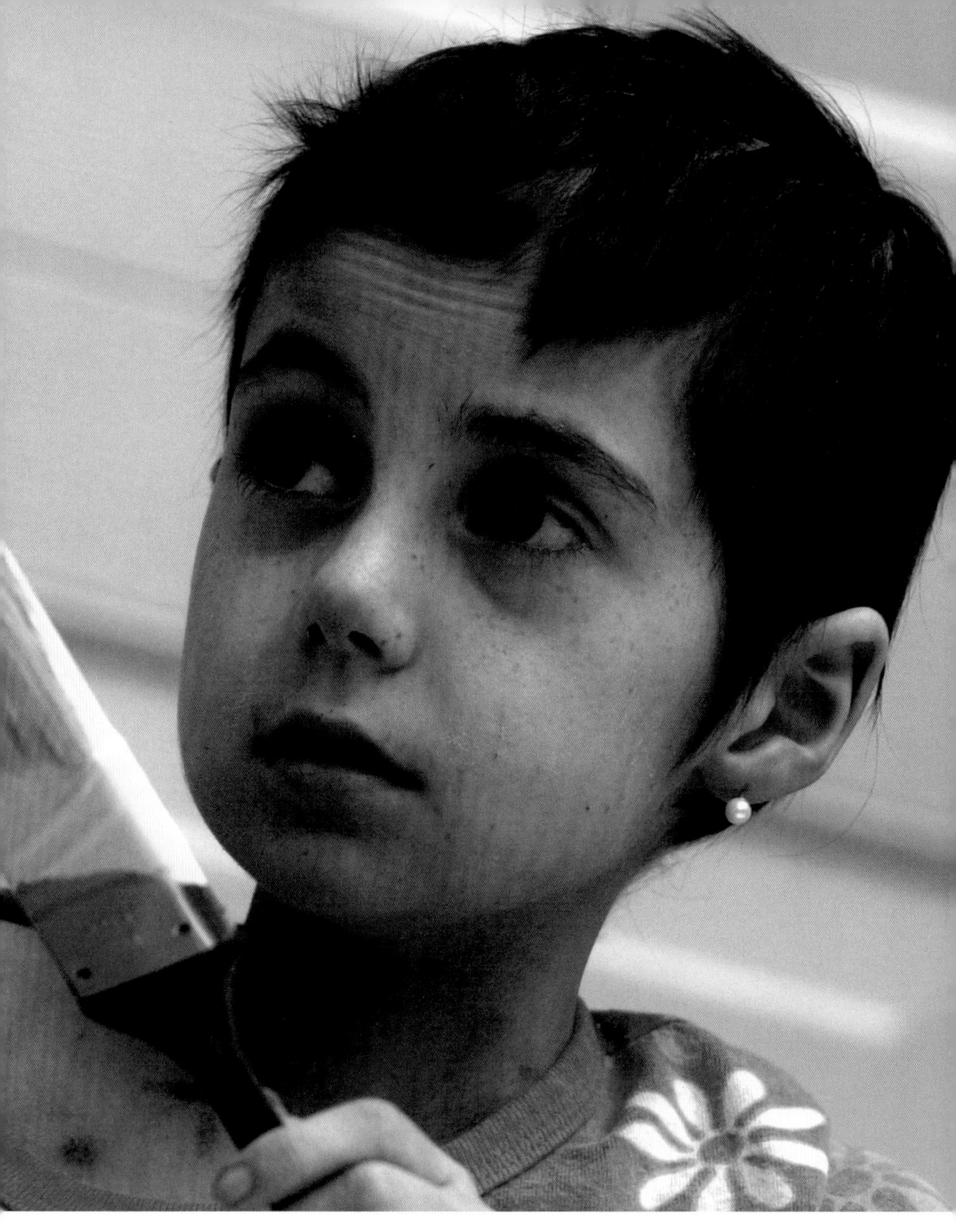

In her short life, Alex inspired millions of people all over the world.

child—even a child four years old and **terminally ill**—can become a hero. As her first lemonade stand proved, no idea, no act of kindness, is ever too small.

Notes

Chapter 1: An Unlikely Hero

1. Liz Scott, telephone interview by author, January 31, 2006.
2. Scott, interview.
3. Quoted in Barry Wigmore, "A Courageous Last Stand," *London Times,* December 8, 2004, p. 7.
4. Scott, interview.
5. Scott, interview.
6. Scott, interview.

Chapter 2: "Maybe They'll Find a Cure"

7. Quoted in Tom Pedulla, "Girl's Message Gallops with Horse," *USA Today,* June 7, 2005, p. C1.
8. Scott, interview.
9. Quoted in Caryl Segalewitz, "Alex's Legacy Lives on in Lemonade Stands," *Dayton (OH) Daily News,* June 6, 2005, p. E2.
10. Quoted in *People,* "In Memoriam: Alex Scott," August 23, 2004, p. 100.
11. Quoted in Jane Clifford "Making a Stand," *San Diego Union-Tribune,* July 23, 2005, p. E1.
12. Quoted in Carrie Budoff, "Girl's Lemonade Stand Helps Cancer Fund," *Hartford Courant,* July 2, 2000, p. B2.

13. Quoted in Budoff, "Girl's Lemonade Stand Helps Cancer Fund," p. B2.
14. Quoted in Budoff, "Girl's Lemonade Stand Helps Cancer Fund," p. B2.
15. Scott, interview.
16. Scott, interview.

Chapter 3: The Idea Grows

17. Quoted in Pedulla, "Girl's Message Gallops with Horse," p. C1.
18. Scott, interview.
19. Quoted in Steve Wartenberg, "More than 1,000 Stop by Alex's Lemonade Stand," *Allentown (PA) Morning Call*, June 13, 2004, p. B1.
20. Quoted in Wartenberg, "More than 1,000 Stop by Alex's Lemonade Stand," p. B1.
21. Quoted in Wigmore, "A Courageous Last Stand," p. 7.
22. Quoted in Wigmore, "A Courageous Last Stand," p. 7.
23. Quoted in Caringbridge, "Journal Entries, Alex Scott." www.caringbridge.com/page/alexscott/index.

Chapter 4: Alex's Legacy

24. Quoted in Ida Berkow, "A Dream in Every Cup," *New York Times*, June 8, 2005, p. D7.
25. Quoted in Nicole Morgan, "Girl's

Lemonade Is Bittersweet," *Norfolk (VA) Virginian*, October 10, 2004, p. B1.

26. Quoted in Clifford, "Making a Stand," p. E1.

Chapter 5: Getting Involved

27. Tracy, personal interview by author, April 2002, New Brighton, MN.
28. Jordan, personal interview by author, April 2002, Minneapolis, MN.
29. Danny, personal interview by author, February 2002, South St. Paul, MN.
30. Lila, telephone interview by author, February 6, 2006.
31. Sara, telephone interview by author, February 12, 2006.
32. Sara, interview.
33. Marissa, telephone interview by author, January 31, 2006.

Glossary

biopsy: The examination of a cutting of a tumor under a microscope to see if it is cancerous.

chemotherapy: A treatment in which powerful drugs are used to kill cancer cells in the body.

fatigue: Extreme tiredness.

humanitarian: For the good of society; for helping people.

intravenous: Given directly into a vein.

MRI scan: A way of looking at the inside of a patient's body without performing surgery.

neuroblastoma: A cancer that starts in the nerve cells of a baby or young child.

optimistic: Hopeful; looking on the bright side.

outpatient: A person who has treatments at a hospital without having to stay overnight.

pediatric: Having to do with children.

philanthropist: A person who works to help other people, such as by raising money for charity.

physical therapist: Someone who helps a patient exercise muscles after an accident or surgery.

radiation therapy: A treatment in which a powerful X-ray is used to try to shrink a tumor.

terminally ill: Very sick from a disease that cannot be cured.

tumor: A growth on or in the body that is sometimes cancerous.

For Further Exploration

Books

Holly Cefrey, *Coping with Cancer.* New York: Rosen, 2000. Good glossary, with interesting chapter on methods of diagnosis.

Alvin Silverstein, *Cancer.* Minneapolis, MN: Twenty-first Century, 2006. Readable text, with an excellent bibliography.

Periodicals

Tom Pedulla, "Girl's Message Gallops with Horse," *USA Today,* June 7, 2005.

Jason Straziuso, "Making a Stand for Research," *Seattle Times,* June 12, 2004.

Web Sites

Alex's Lemonade Stand (www.alexslemonade.org). This site gives complete information about the work of Alex's Lemonade Foundation as well as help for people in starting a stand of their own.

Cancer Kids (http://cancerkids.org). A site that features information about cancer affecting children as well as first-person accounts by young cancer patients and their parents.

Candlelighters (www.candlelighters.org). The

"For Kids" section of this Web site provides links to other sites that deal with specific aspects of pediatric cancer. While most sites are aimed at young cancer patients, there are some that provide help for their parents, siblings, and friends.

Index

Picture Credits

Cover: Alex's Lemonade Stand Foundation
Alex's Lemonade Stand Foundation, 8, 14, 17, 19, 22, 28, 30-31 (all), 32, 45
© Ann Heisenfelt/AP Photo, 21
© Colin Cuthbert/Science Photo Library, 43
© CORBIS, 47
© Ed Eckstein/CORBIS, 24
© Hal Smith, The Emporia Gazette/AP Photo, 48-49
© Jacqueline Larma/AP Photo, 7, 34-35, 51-52
© Jennifer Graylock/AP Photo, 27
© Lester Lefkowitz/CORBIS, 11
© Matt Sullivan/Reuters/CORBIS, 38-39
© Molly Riley/Reuters/CORBIS, 40
© Roger Ressmeyer/CORBIS, 50
© Simon Fraser/Royal Victoria Infirmary, Newcastle/Science Photo Library, 12

About the Author

Gail B. Stewart received her undergraduate degree from Gustavus Adolphus College in St. Peter, Minnesota. She did her graduate work in English, linguistics, and curriculum study at the College of St. Thomas and the University of Minnesota. She taught English and reading for more than ten years.

She has written over ninety books for young people, including a series for Lucent Books called The Other America. She has written many books on historical topics such as World War I and the Warsaw ghetto.

Stewart and her husband live in Minneapolis with their three sons, Ted, Elliot, and Flynn; two dogs; and a cat. When Stewart is not writing, she enjoys reading, walking, and watching her sons play soccer.